RUBANK EDUCATIONAL LIBRARY No. 79

Soloist Folio

FOR

Eb OR F HORN (FRENCH HORN - ALTO - MELLOPHONE)

with Piano Accompaniment

CONTENTS

RUBANK®

HAL•LEONARD® CORPORATION

7777 W. BLUEMOUND RD. P.O. BOX 13819 MILWAUKEE, WI 53213

Shenandoah
(Across the Wide Missouri)

F Horn

CHANTY
Arr. by Clarence E. Hurrell

Adagio
from Der Freischütz

F Horn

C. M. VON WEBER
Arr. by G. E. Holmes

Shenandoah
(Across the Wide Missouri)

Eb Horn
Eb Alto or Mellophone

CHANTY
Arr. by Clarence E. Hurrell

Adagio
from Der Freischütz

Eb Horn
Eb Alto or Mellophone

C. M. VON WEBER
Arr. by G. E. Holmes

Andante Cantabile

from Fifth Symphony

F Horn

P. TSCHAIKOWSKY
Arr. by G. E. Holmes

Andante Cantabile

from Fifth Symphony

Eb Horn
Eb Alto or Mellophone

P. TSCHAIKOWSKY
Arr. by G.E. Holmes

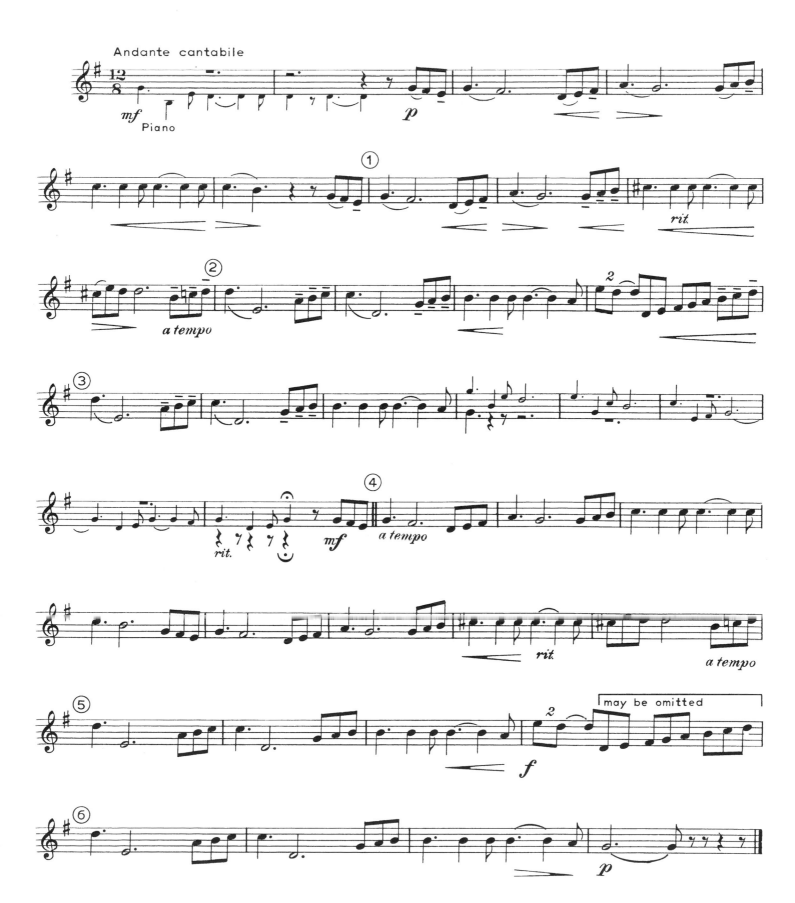

632-16

Liebesträume
(Dreams of Love)

F Horn

FRANZ LISZT
Arr. by G. E. Holmes

Andante
from Concerto, Op. 64

F Horn

F. MENDELSSOHN
Arr. by G. E. Holmes

Liebesträume
(Dreams of Love)

Eb Horn
Eb Alto or Mellophone

FRANZ LISZT
Arr. by G. E. Holmes

Andante
from Concerto, Op. 64

Eb Horn
Eb Alto or Mellophone

F. MENDELSSOHN
Arr. by G. E. Holmes

Copyright MCMXXXIX by Rubank, Inc., Chicago, Ill.
International Copyright Secured
Copyright Renewed

Introduction to Third Act
from Lohengrin

F Horn

R. WAGNER
Arr. by G. E. Holmes

Introduction to Third Act
from Lohengrin

Eb Horn
Eb Alto or Mellophone

R. WAGNER
Arr. by G. E. Holmes

Poem

F Horn

Z. FIBICH
Arr. by G. E. Holmes

Home on the Range

F Horn

AMERICAN COWBOY SONG
Arr. by G. E. Holmes

632-16

RUBANK EDUCATIONAL LIBRARY No. 79

Soloist Folio

FOR

Eb OR F HORN (FRENCH HORN - ALTO - MELLOPHONE)

with Piano Accompaniment

CONTENTS

RUBANK®

HAL•LEONARD®
CORPORATION
7777 W. BLUEMOUND RD. P.O. Box 13819 MILWAUKEE, WI 53213

Shenandoah
(Across the Wide Missouri)

CHANTY
Arr. by Clarence E. Hurrell

633-27

Adagio
from Der Freischütz

C. M. VON WEBER
Arr. by G. E. Holmes

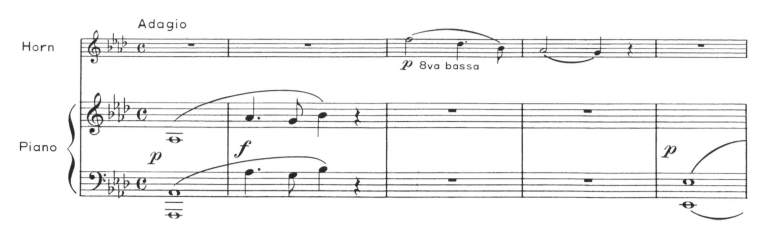

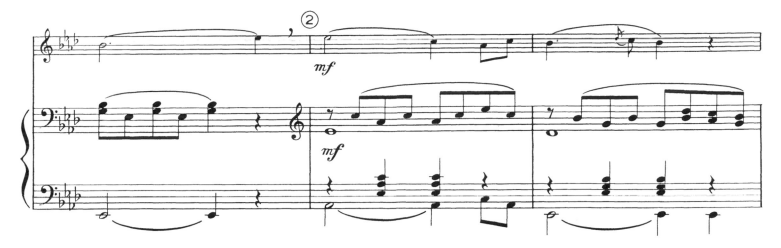

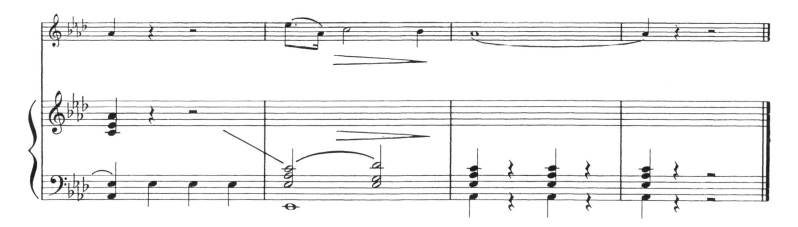

Andante Cantabile
from Fifth Symphony

P. TSCHAIKOWSKY
Arr. by G. E. Holmes

633-27

8

633 - 27

Liebesträume
(Dreams of Love)

FRANZ LISZT
Arr. by G. E. Holmes

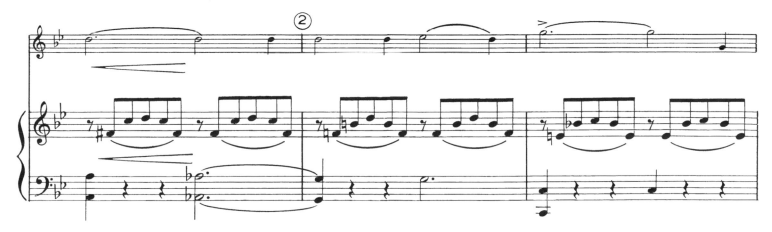

633-27

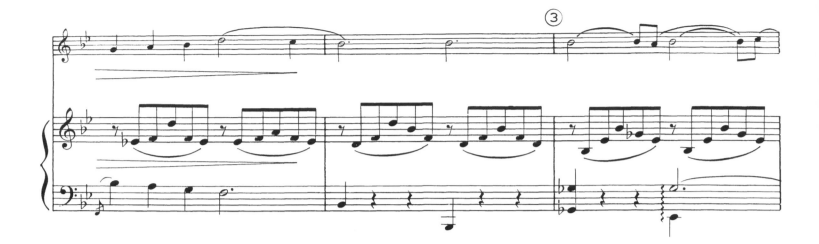

poco cresc. ed agitato

poco cresc ed agitato

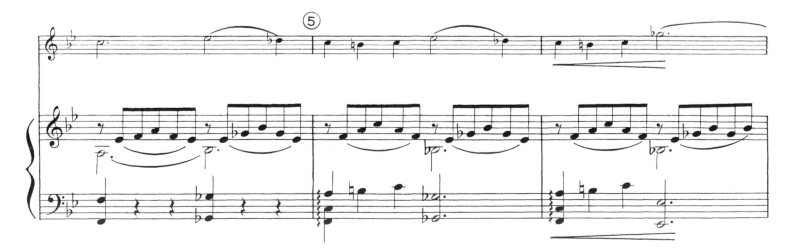

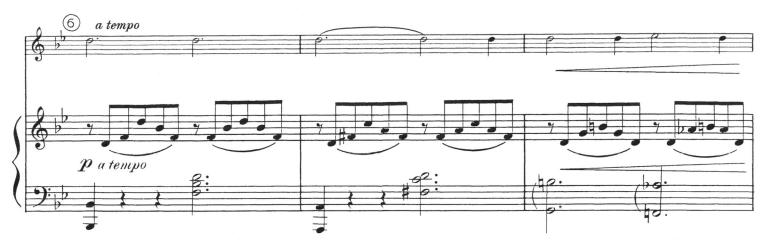

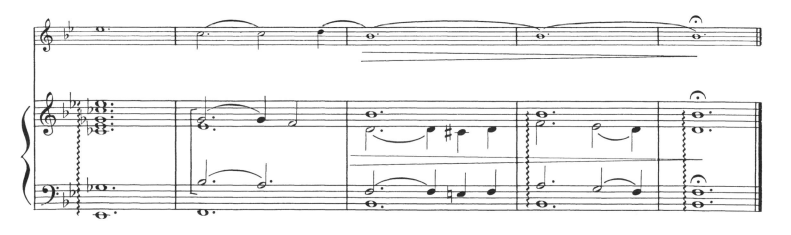

633 - 27

Andante
from Concerto, Op, 64

F. MENDELSSOHN
Arr. by G. E. Holmes

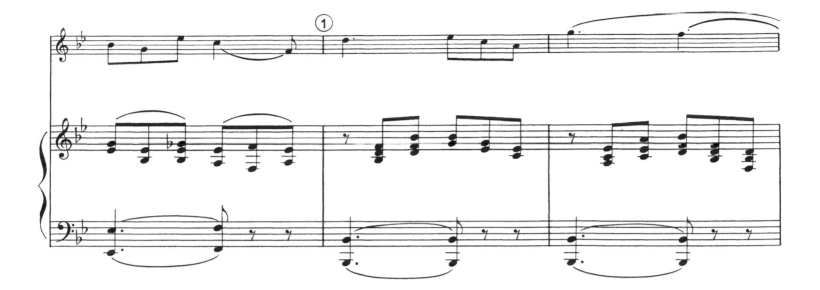

633-27

Introduction to Third Act
from Lohengrin

R. WAGNER
Arr. by G. E. Holmes

633-27

This Page Left Blank

To eliminate unnecessary turning of pages while performing the succeeding compositions . . .

—The Publisher

Poem

Z. FIBICH
Arr. by G.E. Holmes

633-27

Home on the Range

AMERICAN COWBOY SONG
Arr. by G. E. Holmes

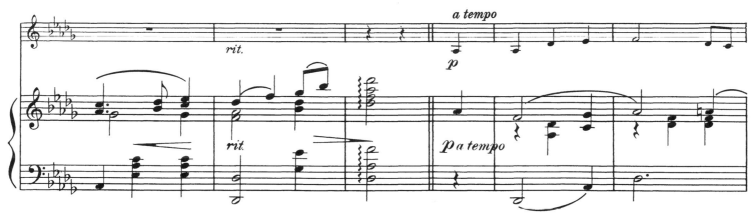

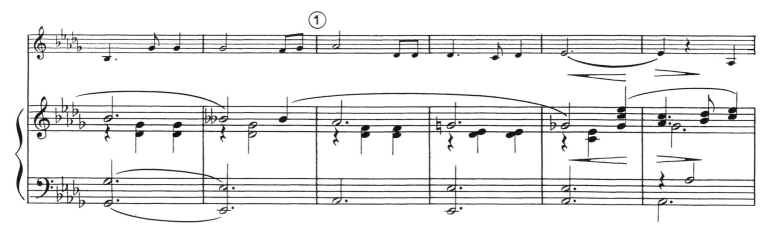

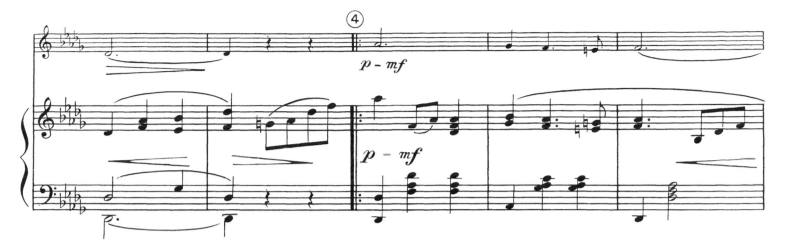

Sing, Smile, Slumber
Berceuse

CHARLES GOUNOD
Arr. by G. E. Holmes

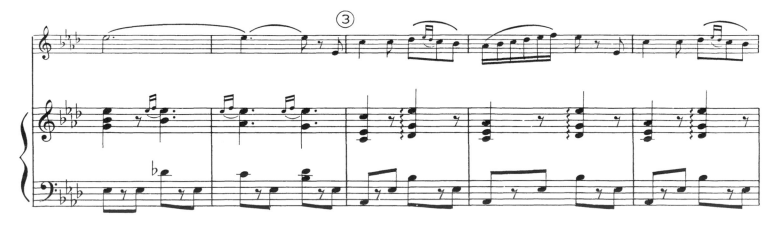

Sarabanda and Gavotta

A. CORELLI
Arr. by Clarence E. Hurrell

Allegro moderato

Bohemian Girl
(Melodies)

W. BALFE
Arr. by G. E. Holmes

Horn

Piano

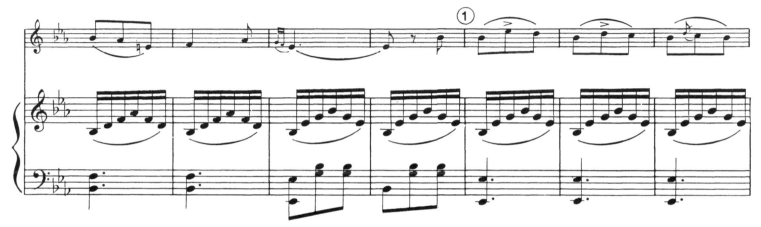

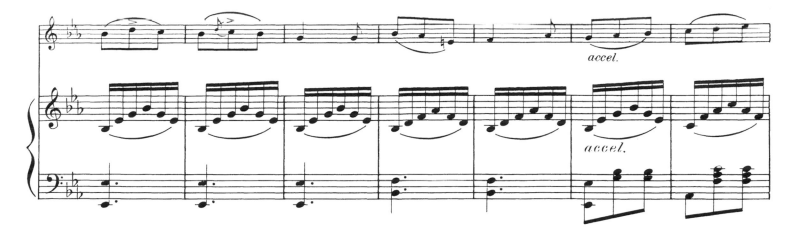

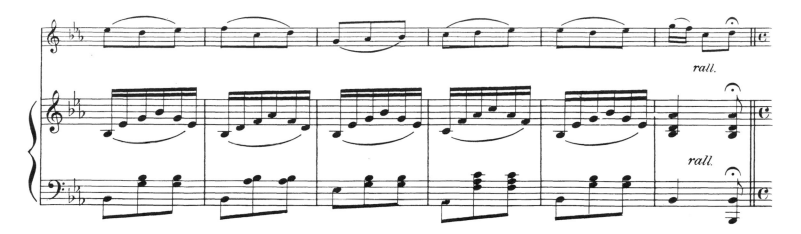

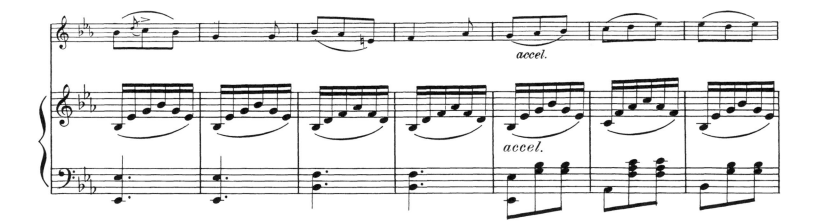

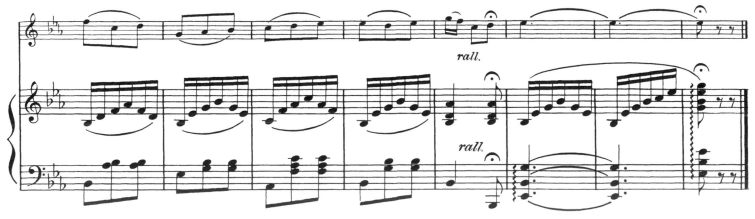

The Victor

R. M. ENDRESEN

633-27

Poem

Eb Horn
Eb Alto or Mellophone

Z. FIBICH
Arr. by G. E. Holmes

Home on the Range

Eb Horn
Eb Alto or Mellophone

AMERICAN COWBOY SONG
Arr. by G. E. Holmes

Sing, Smile, Slumber
Berceuse

F Horn

CHARLES GOUNOD
Arr. by G. E. Holmes

Moderato
Piano

632-16

Sing, Smile, Slumber

Berceuse

Eb Horn
Eb Alto or Mellophone

CHARLES GOUNOD
Arr. by G. E. Holmes

Moderato
Piano

632-16

Sarabanda and Gavotta

F Horn

A. CORELLI
Arr. by Clarence E. Hurrell

Sarabanda and Gavotta

Eb Horn
Eb Alto or Mellophone

A. CORELLI
Arr. by Clarence E. Hurrell

Bohemian Girl
(Melodies)

F Horn

W. BALFE
Arr. by G. E. Holmes

Bohemian Girl
(Melodies)

Eb Horn
Eb Alto or Mellophone

W. BALFE
Arr. by G. E. Holmes

632-16

The Victor

F Horn

R. M. ENDRESEN

632-16

The Victor

Eb Horn
Eb Alto or Mellophone

R. M. ENDRESEN

632-16